AMERICAN ECLIPSES

FLAVIA PANKIEWICZ

Translated by PETER CARRAVETTA

With an Introductory Note by JOSEPH TUSIANI

BORDIGHERA
WEST LAFAYETTE, IN

Library of Congress Cataloging-in-Publication Data

Pankiewicz, Flavia.
  [Eclissi americane. English]
  American Eclipses / Flavia Pankiewicz ; translated by Peter Carravetta, with an introductory note by Joseph Tusiani.
   p.   cm. — (Crossings ; 4)
  ISBN 1-884419-23-2
  1. Italian—Travel—New York (State—New York Poetry.
2. Italians—Travel—United States Poetry. 3. New York (N.Y.) Poetry. 4. United States Poetry. I. Carravetta, Peter. II. Title. III. Series: Crossings (West Lafayette, Ind.) ; 4.
PQ4876.A465E28 1999
851 '.914—dc21   99-28928
                                                         CIP

Cover graphics: Carlo Conversano

Layout: Alberto De Donno

Cover photo: "Moon over Manhattan" by Santi Visalli, courtesy of the
       photographer

© 1999 by Flavia Pankiewicz, Italian Poetry
© 1999 by Peter Carravetta, English Translation
© 1999 by Joseph Tusiani, Introduction

All rights reserved. Parts of this book may be reprinted only by written permission from the editors, and may not be reproduced for publication in book, magazine, or electronic media of any kind, except in quotations for purposes of literary reviews by critics.

Printed in the United States.

Published by
BORDIGHERA PRESS
Purdue University
1359 Stanley Coulter Hall
West Lafayette, IN 47907-1359

CROSSINGS 4
ISBN 1-884419-23-2

*Dedicated to the memory
of my father
and my aunt Julia.
It is to them,
through an involved chain
of circumstances,
that I owe my encounter
with the American Land*

TABLE OF CONTENTS

Introductory Note by Joseph Tusiani   7

I
NEW YORK 549 DAYS AND 18 MINUTES

Triborough Bridge	10
April	14
Midtown Manhattan	16
Greenwich Village	18
New York Public Library	20
Pathways	22
Water	24
Rain	28
Hudson River	32
City Island	34
February	36

II
AMERICAN ECLIPSES

Exodus	40
The Beasts in the Temple	42
The Sales Clerk at the Emporium	46
Traps	48
Poison	50
American Eclipses	52

Biographical Notes   59

Introductory Note

Quick, white-heat notes. Notes which, once jotted down in a magic notebook, become starting-points for high lyricism.

Like all visitors Flavia Pankiewicz is enchanted by the ineffable, polyhedric character of New York, but, almost instinctively, only she can explain the charm to herself and to us. Every corner of this metropolis sparks off in her memories or visions of an ancestral world, that, strangely, is the one in which we live, so "the unreal is real, / the real unreal." In Midtown Manhattan, on the Triborough Bridge, at City Island, by the Hudson River, as far as the New York Public Library, the same sense of awe leans onto a solid base of unforgotten contrasts: "what's not there for the wretched of the earth. / Desire to invent heaven for them. / For you."

It is particularly in the short lyric poem *The Sales Clerk at the Emporium* that Pankiewicz enjoys and brings to life the moment of her most concise and aery poetry. Imagine a tourist walking into this typically American store holding a careful list of things to buy: flippers, a raft, sunglasses, a sail, rope, an anchor, water and food and, just in case, hammer, nails and wood. The salesman hands

hands over the items one by one, but is too busy, or maybe too American to hear the excited Greek chorus that makes a background comment to the handing over of every single article. Flippers: "I have to swim across the ocean." Raft: "to save me from the tug of the currents." Sunglasses: "so I won't see the sun anymore, so it won't blind me." A sail: "that takes to the wind towards secure shore." And so on, leading to the unexpected revelation-liberation: "a few strewn shells, / after the landing, / will celebrate the shipwreck forever."

The reading of these pages brings to mind transfigurations, rather than photographs. The title of the first part of the collection has, therefore, a lyrical quality in itself. It doesn't speak of nearly two years, but of 549 days and 18 minutes, because every day, every minute, is an extraordinary intimate event.

It is this analytical observation of the passing of time that enables the poet to perceive, and halt in her soul, the vicissitudes of time itself – the momentary darkness that will engender a brighter and more glorious radiance. Such *Eclipses* are, so to speak, more easily visible from American soil, but they span from sky to sky.

Joseph Tusiani

I
NEW YORK 549 DAYS AND 18 MINUTES

In vain we attempt to elude
the noise of water
or the song of birds.
The uncanny is in our soul.

Taisen Deshimaru
Zen Master

La poesia viene da Dio.
È solo Dio che regala emozioni.

TRIBOROUGH BRIDGE

Dove comincia la vita,
prima della Creazione,
nella notte universale,
galleggia Manhattan
come un sogno di luci
che sconfiggono il buio.
Si libra
evanescente, onirica,
fuori dal tempo.
In un futuro remoto
scivola il presente.
La notte dei tempi si scioglie
nell'isola che galleggia sul nulla.
Il Potere che sfida i cieli,
Dio che regala visioni.
Svetta Manhattan
scintillante come un diamante,
lontana dalle umane miserie,
fedele soltanto al Sogno.
S'innalza, scorre, si protende,
come una visione di speranza,
di speranze, di infinito.
Sognare o possedere.

*Poetry comes from God. Only
God makes of emotion a gift.*

TRIBOROUGH BRIDGE

Where life begins,
before Creation,
in the universal night,
there Manhattan floats
like a light-filled dream
defeating the darkness.
It hovers
evanescent, dreamy,
outside time.
The present slips away
into a remote future.
The mist of time dissolves
on the island floating in nothingness.
The Power that challenges the skies,
God giving away visions.
Manhattan stands out
shining like a diamond,
far from human miseries,
loyal only to the Dream.
It rises, flows, lurches forward,
like a vision of hope,
full of hopes, of endlessness.
To dream or to possess.

Essere, essere per sempre.
Trascendere.
Questa è Manhattan:
Pilastro dell'Universo,
Crocevia di Esistenze,
Monumento di Sfida.
Luce e ancora Luce che galleggia nel buio,
Principio Universale.
Questa è Manhattan
che ho visto dal Triborough Bridge,
in una notte di ottobre,
prima che Dio creasse il mondo.

Being, being forever.
Transcending.
This is Manhattan:
Pillar of the Universe,
Crossroads of Existences,
Monument of the Quest.
Light and more Light floating in the darkness.
Universal Principle.
This is Manhattan
as I saw it from the Triborough Bridge,
one October night,
before God created the world.

APRILE

Aprile è inquieto.
Aprile è perverso.
Aprile è luminoso.
Aprile è un'attesa.
Aprile è un segnale.
Aprile è un profeta.
L'aria è densa,
l'oscurità è tiepida,
tutto scorre.
Dipinti astratti a Soho
come catene intrecciate che non si incontrano.
Spazi circoscritti a Soho
incrociano i destini
come un gioco di perle di vetro.
Sfere inconsapevoli che si sfiorano,
traiettorie ancora incerte
– già definite? – del futuro.
Sguardi e parole.
Niente. Tutto.
Niente. Qualcosa.
Tracciati. Linee tracciate verso un futuro
che avanza con prepotenza.
Aprile è un dono.
Aprile è il nuovo.
Aprile è un principio.
New York è assorta.
La sera è andata.
Le immagini restano.
Il fiume scorre.

APRIL

April is restless.
April is perverse.
April is bright.
April is a wait.
April is a sign.
April is a prophet.
The air is thick,
the darkness is warm,
everything flows.
Abstract paintings in Soho
like intertwined chains that never touch.
Confined spaces in Soho
criss cross destinies
like a game of glass pearls.
Spheres unawares barely touching,
trajectories still uncertain
– already established? – of their future.
Glances and words.
Nothing. Everything.
Nothing. Something.
Layouts. Lines sketching a future
that proceeds unflinchingly.
April is a gift.
April is what's new.
April is a beginning.
New York is thoughtful.
The evening is gone.
The images remain.
The river flows.

MIDTOWN MANHATTAN

42nd Street,
torri di cristallo,
una finestra su New York,
profilo di città universo che gela il sangue
nella bellezza piatta del primo sole pomeridiano.
La stanza è inondata di luce
e ci sono solo parole.
Parole,
e fiumi sotterranei in cui germogliano semi
e oscure caverne del cuore
dove si nutrono speranze senza forma.
Futuro incastonato in un presente inconsapevole.
Manhattan toglie il respiro.
È bella, d'una bellezza inspiegabile
l'inconsapevolezza della vita.

MIDTOWN MANHATTAN

42nd Street,
crystal towers,
a window on New York,
the profile of a universe city freezing the blood
in the flat beauty of the early afternoon sun.
The room is bathed in light
and there is only words.
Words,
and underground rivers where seeds bloom
and obscure caves of the heart
where shapeless hopes nourish themselves.
Future mounted in an unwitting present.
Manhattan takes your breath away.
It's beautiful, of an inexplicable beauty
the unawareness of life.

GREENWICH VILLAGE

Dolce. Dolce. Dolce.
Fragole con panna e cioccolato
a Greenwich Village.
Colore, folclore, bohème
che scorre lungo le strade.
L'amore: non c'entra.
La vita: non c'entra.
Qui il lavoro meccanico
si concentra
in un piccolo tavolo di dolcezze
e cioccolato,
buono, buonissimo,
bello, bellissimo,
caldo.
Parlare è il luogo più sicuro del mondo.
Bene, benissimo,
troppo bene.
L'amore non c'entra.
La vita non c'entra.
Troppo bello. Troppo sicuro.

GREENWICH VILLAGE

Sweet. Sweet. Sweet.
Strawberries with cream and chocolate
in Greenwich Village.
Color, folklore, Boheme
coursing through the streets.
Love: not a part of it.
Life: not a part of it.
Here the mechanics of work
can be seen
on a tiny table of kindness
and chocolate,
good, so good,
beautiful, so beautiful,
hot.
Speaking is the safest place on earth.
Well, very well,
too well.
Love's got nothing to do with it.
Life's got nothing to do with it.
Too beautiful. Too sure.

NEW YORK PUBLIC LIBRARY

Mille libri. Mille anni di storia.
Mille e mille parole.
Poliedri di teorie.
Parallelepipedi di dati.
Storia che si attorciglia,
pozzi profondi di pensieri e sudore.
Per niente. Per caso. Per fede.
E scrivere. E non dormire.
E scrivere ancora.
Prende forma il pensiero.
Si materializza.
Fluisce. In una sola direzione.
Tutto converge. Tutto.
I grandi pensatori. I piccoli protagonisti.
Gli oppressi del mondo.
Quelli che vogliamo salvare.
Quelli da riscattare.
Pagheremmo con la vita.
Voglia di rivoluzione.
Ansia di combattere l'ingiustizia.
Di scovarla. Di accopparla.
Di restituire alla vita equilibrio e bellezza.
Quello che non c'è per i dannati della terra.
Voglia di creare paradisi per loro.
Per te.

NEW YORK PUBLIC LIBRARY

Thousands of books. A thousand years of history.
Thousands upon thousands of words.
A multiplicity of theories.
Pyramids of data.
History coiling upon itself,
deep wells of thoughts and sweat.
For nothing. By chance. In trust.
And writing. And no sleep.
And keep on writing.
Thinking taking shape.
It comes to life.
It flows. One way.
Everything comes together. Everything.
The great thinkers. The little guys.
The oppressed of the world.
Those we mean to save.
Those to redeem.
It would cost us our lives.
A longing for revolution.
Eagerness to fight injustice.
To snuff it out. To slay it.
To restore balance and beauty to life yet again.
What's not there for the wretched of the earth.
Desire to invent heaven for them.
For you.

PERCORSI

Una nuova primavera
ha ravvivato i cieli con pennellate di luce.
Si dipanano le esistenze
e New York è di nuovo assolata,
afosa, globale, assordante;
non fa sentire il rumore del fiume,
dell'acqua,
che scorre.
Il fluire del sangue,
le scariche elettriche della mente,
attenuate, ingabbiate, soppresse
dal grande ventre di Manhattan.
Rumore assordante che impedisce
di ascoltare il battito del cuore.
Città, città universo,
il traffico come pensiero,
semafori come tappe di vita.
Rumori e suoni stereofonici della città
annientano
il sapore pieno, inebriante,
di dolcissima cioccolata.

PATHWAYS

A new Spring
has rekindled the skies with brushstrokes of light.
Lives untangle
and New York is once again sundrenched,
thick, global, deafening;
you cannot hear the river,
the water,
flowing.
The coursing of blood,
the electric discharges of the mind
are dampened, caged, suppressed
by the great bosom of Manhattan.
Deafening noise that impairs
listening to heartbeats.
City, universe city,
traffic as thinking,
traffic lights as life stages.
Noises and stereo sounds of the city
which annihilate
the full, intoxicating flavor
of sweet chocolate.

ACQUA

Io non mi ricordo
se erano fiumi, montagne o mari.
Io non so più
se era a New York o altrove
ma il centro dell'universo erano le ore;
tempo metafisico scandito
non più in ere, stagioni o giorni
ma in ore, ore, quante ore,
lunghe ore, rapide come un battito d'ali,
incise per sempre come un solco profondo in una roccia.
Roccia, caverna o cavità del mondo
dove tutto inizia,
nelle viscere della terra,
le sorgenti dei fiumi
che alimentano il mare,
che nutrono l'oceano,
principio della vita.
È una goccia d'acqua l'inizio di tutto,
acqua primordiale ed eterna,
acqua per sempre,
conduttrice di elettricità,
scariche che si fanno tuono e tempesta,
tempesta.
Cervello e cuore e sangue.
Tempesta.

Tutto è leggero.
Tutto è spensierato.
Il tempo non esiste.

WATER

I can't quite tell anymore
whether they were rivers or mountains or seas.
I don't know anymore
if we were in New York or some other place
but the center of the universe were the hours;
metaphysical time no longer partitioned
in eras or seasons or days
but rather in hours, hours, so many hours,
long hours, speeding like fluttering wings,
forever carved in stone like a deep groove.
Rock, cave or hollow of the world
where everything begins,
in the gut of the earth,
springs for rivers
that feed the seas,
that feed the ocean,
origin of life.
It took a drop of water to get everything started,
primordial and eternal water,
water forever,
bearing electricity,
sparks that become thunder and tempest,
a storm.
Mind and heart and blood.
A storm.

Everything is light.
Everything is carefree.
Time vanishes.

Il mondo non esiste.
Sole, sole e colore. Colore e sole.
Inebriante come una cascata di petali di rose.
Bello come il dipinto di un artista sublime.
Sfarzoso come un sogno.
Come un sogno, breve.
Azzurro. Azzurro. E verde.
E cieli e orizzonti spalancati.
E un volo bianco di gabbiani
a solcare gli azzurri.
E un tremito di vele
a squarciare i verdi.
Indimenticabile.
Scivolare, scivolare in movimento perpetuo,
pianeta che gira,
evoluzioni della mente, dei sensi.
Volare, librarsi in alto,
solo per ritornare a questo scoglio.
Alberi e ombre accoglienti,
profumi di resine, da attraversare in fretta,
senza lasciarsi soggiogare.
E l'acqua, ancora una volta l'acqua,
dove tutto è iniziato,
a cui tutto ritorna.
Silenzi.
Pensieri.
Attraversare il mondo senza toccarlo.
Profumi avvolgenti da cui non lasciarsi ammaliare.
Gabbie della mente
per continuare marce parallele.
Per sempre. Per ora.

The world disappears.
Sun, sun and color. Color and sun.
Intoxicating like a cascade of rose petals.
Beautiful like a painting by a sublime artist.
Sumptuous like a dream.
And like a dream, fleeting.
Blue. Blue. And green.
Wide open skies and horizons.
And a white flight of seagulls
slicing through the blue.
And a quivering of sails
tearing through the green.
Unforgettable.
Sliding, sliding in perpetual motion,
like a revolving planet,
evolving like the mind, like the senses.
Flying, hovering up high,
only to alight on this rock.
Welcoming trees and shadows,
the smell of resins, crossing in a hurry,
without yielding to any incantation.
And water, the water once again,
where it all began,
where it all returns.
Silences.
Thoughts.
Crossing the world without touching it.
Sweeping aromas to fend off.
Mental grids
so to continue parallel paths.
For ever. For the time being.

PIOGGIA

Legno che scricchiola sotto i tacchi,
la casa è tiepida e asciutta;
fuori, il mondo è bagnato,
intriso di pioggia.
Pioggia.
La realtà non è stata nient'altro
nelle ultime dodici ore.
Ha bagnato gli alberi, intriso la terra, inondato le strade,
ha avvolto le case, ha reso di spugna le foglie,
morbida e costante, ha travolto ogni cosa nel suo lento fluire
quassù, tra le colline del Westchester.
Acqua e buio,
fuori non c'è nient'altro
e nel cuore solo una piccola speranza
che magicamente, d'un tratto, si materializza.

E la pioggia diventa sipario, palcoscenico, set
e il varco di un ombrello è un corridoio perfetto
tra il nulla e la felicità.
Impermeabili sgualciti e sorrisi,
la gente sembra irreale,
come in un sogno,
intorno al fuoco,
come in un sogno,
gente bellissima,
come in un sogno.

Una piccola candela
illumina di luce del tutto nuova

RAIN

Wood creaking beneath the heels.
The house is warm and dry;
outside, the world is wet,
drenched by the rain.
Rain.
Reality has been nothing but
during the past twelve hours.
It has soaked the trees, dampened the earth, flooded the streets,
it has enveloped the houses, turned the leaves to sponges,
soft and steadfast, overrunning everything in its sluggish flow
up here, in the hills of Westchester County.
Water and darkness,
nothing else outside
while in my heart there's a ray of hope
which suddenly, as if by magic, comes to life.

And the rain becomes a curtain, a stage, a set
and the passage cut by the umbrella is a perfect corridor
between nothing and happiness.
Wrinkled raincoats between smiles,
people seem unreal,
as in a dream,
around the fire,
as in a dream,
beautiful people,
as in a dream.

A small candle
burns with a new kind of light

i vecchi ricordi
e i diari rinascono dal fuoco
che li ha resi cenere,
e i morti resuscitano
e il passato rivive,
vivo e irreale come il presente.
E il Tappan Zee e il George Washington Bridge,
dileguati nelle foschie della pioggia,
ricompaiono
con profili di fiammelle
che scandiscono traiettorie nel buio.
Perfetto, troppo perfetto.
L'irreale è reale,
il reale irreale.
Magico.
Incastonato nel tempo finito.
Tassello essenziale o irrisorio frammento
ma perfetto.
E per sempre.

the old memories
and the diaries are brought back to life by the fire
that had turned them to ashes,
and the dead come back to life
and the past lives again,
alive and unreal like the present.
And the Tappan Zee and the George Washington Bridge
vanish in the haze of the rain,
then reappear
like profiles of tiny flames
that draw pathways in the darkness.
Perfect, too perfect.
The unreal is real,
the real unreal.
Magic.
Mounted in a finite time.
Essential stupple or insignificant fragment
yet perfect.
And forever.

HUDSON RIVER

Notte sull'Hudson River,
sotto la luna,
su una panchina,
davanti all'acqua.
Notte di ghiaia ed erba sotto i piedi.
Notte di legno umido.
Notte di tappeti di foglie secche.
Il fiume è scuro e placido
come un gigante addormentato.
Notte tiepida, senza freddo.
Notte immobile e silenziosa,
fuori dal tempo.
Il fiume è davanti
e tutto intorno
e nella mente.
La luna è pallida,
la luce è lattea,
il buio è chiarore.
Sponde dolcissime e silenziose.
Acqua vicina, vicinissima.
Passi e silenzi,
silenzi e parole e parole.
In un cono di luce,
in una infinitesimale porzione di universo,
l'Eden è una sfera.

HUDSON RIVER

A night on the banks of the Hudson,
under the moon,
on a park bench,
by the water.
Night of pebbles and grass under foot.
Night of soaked wood.
Night carpeted with fallen leaves.
The river is dark and calm
like a sleeping giant.
Tepid night, not at all cold.
Still and silent night,
beyond time.
The river is before us
and all around
and in the mind.
The moon is pale,
the light is milky,
the darkness luminescent.
The banks are quiet and mellow.
The water nearby, very close.
Steps and silences,
silences and words.
In a cone of light,
in a minuscule corner of the cosmos,
Eden is a sphere.

CITY ISLAND

Una lingua di terra protesa sull'acqua
e le luci dei ristoranti
luccicano
parallele alla geometria perfetta della strada.
L'acqua grigia del Long Island Sound
è blu inchiostro in una notte di luna piena
e le lanterne delle barche sono chimere.
Cercando un tavolo con *water view*
scegliere un luogo, come in un gioco.
Parlarsi è un film,
raccontarsi è un copione.
Lui è cortese.
Lui è crudele.
Lui è disponibile.
Lui è ambiguo.
Lui è perfetto.
Lei è incerta.
Lei è dolce.
Lei è turbata.
Lei è ferita.
Lei è felice.
Li ho visti andare via abbracciati,
nella notte di City Island,
a dirsi bugie,
a rivelarsi verità,
a caccia di emozioni,
avidi di illusioni,
scettici e ingenui,
dubbiosi e caparbi.
Il buio ha fatto il resto.
La notte ha suggellato una promessa.

CITY ISLAND

A tongue of land jutting into the water
and the restaurant lights
twinkling
in parallel with the perfect geometry of the avenue.
The grey water of the Long Island Sound
is like blue ink under the full moon
while the lanterns from the boats are chimeras.
Looking for a table with a water view
choosing the place as in a game.
Speaking to each other is a film,
telling each other's story is a script.
He is courteous.
He is cruel.
He is available.
He is ambivalent.
He is perfect.
She is unsure.
She is sweet.
She is uneasy.
She is wounded.
She is happy.
I saw them leaving in an embrace,
in a City Island night,
telling each other lies,
revealing truths
while hunting for emotions,
thirsting for illusions,
skeptical and naive,
doubtful and pigheaded.
The darkness did the rest.
The night sealed a promise.

FEBBRAIO

Freddo e razionale
il disegno non ha più alcun senso.
Tempo e silenzi.
Le sfere emanano solo emozioni da ricordare.
Ma il fiume è maestro e scorre.
L'Hudson è stato il mio Gange.

FEBRUARY

Cold yet rational
the sketch makes no longer sense.
Time and silences.
The spheres issue forth only emotions to remember.
But the river is master and it flows.
The Hudson was my Ganges.

II

AMERICAN ECLIPSES

ESODO

Andarsene da se stessi,
strappare radici,
amputarsi le braccia
e andarsene.
Lasciare le luminose terre promesse
per nebbie pallide e pacate.
Troncare. Dimenticare.
Fare la vita a pezzetti
e buttare il superfluo.
Tuffarsi nel profondo dell'anima
a cercare la perla preziosa:
disfarsi della chincaglieria,
subito.
Chincaglieria abbagliante come gemma,
fatua come il vapore dei tombini di New York,
sterile come un sogno stupefacente,
piena di fascino,
del fascino d'un travestito.
A che serve inebriarsi
di divinità dell'antica Grecia,
osannare crocifissi
o invocare Buddha?
La terra si è inaridita sotto il peso
della sua leggerezza.
Tutte le luci di Manhattan si sono spente.
Long Island è sprofondata nell'oceano senza lasciare traccia.
I suoi abitanti sono partiti.
L'esodo è completo.

EXODUS

Leaving oneself behind,
tearing one's roots,
cutting one's arms off
and go away.
Leaving luminous promised lands
for pale and pacific fogs.
Ending it. Forgetting.
Cutting life up into bits
and throwing away what is unnecessary.
Leaping into the depths of the soul
in search of a precious pearl;
getting rid of all the paraphernalia,
quickly.
Paraphernalia that blind like a gem,
fatuous like the vapor from New York manholes,
fruitless like hallucinating dreams,
richly fascinating,
with the fascination of a transvestite.
What's the use of getting drunk
on ancient Greek divinities,
celebrate crucifixes
or call out to the Buddha?
The earth turned arid under the weight
of its own lightness.
All the lights in Manhattan are out.
Long Island just plunged into the Ocean without a trace.
Its inhabitants are gone.
The exodus is complete.

BELVE NEL TEMPIO

Manhattan è un tempio
e le strade sono navate
e moloch i grattacieli.
Gli altari laterali delle sue costruzioni
si stagliano contro cieli friabili.
Il traffico è acqua di fiume,
il Village è un estuario.
Manhattan è un flipper,
e che altro?
Un videogioco impazzito
in cui si mescolano le essenze del mondo.
Ma i suoi cieli da oggi
sono solcati da aquile
e non più da colombe.
E le tigri corrono libere per le sue strade
in cerca di prede.
Avanzano, assetate di sangue, le pantere.
Incombono, spavaldi, i leoni,
pronti a donare, con gli artigli, la morte.
Invochiamo una giustizia che plachi la sete,
che medichi le ferite con unguenti magici,
che ricomponga i brandelli di carne strappati,
che resusciti i morti,
che ci renda la vita eterna.
Lo zoo postmoderno è esploso per disintegrare il colore.
I terremoti hanno minato i pilastri dell'isola.
Si salvano gli ultimi venditori di hamburger,
i coreani con le loro collezioni di frutta variopinta
e quel negro solitario che suona la tromba sulla Quinta Strada.

THE BEASTS IN THE TEMPLE

Manhattan is a temple,
the streets are naves,
the skyscrapers molochs.
The side altars of its building
are stark against the shifty skies.
Traffic is water from the river,
the Village is an estuary.
Manhattan is a flipper,
what else could it be?
A videogame run amock
that reshuffles the essences of life.
But starting today its skies
will be plied by eagles
no longer by doves.
And the tigers will roam freely the streets
in search of prey.
Bloodthirsty panthers inch forward.
And proud lions prowl the area,
ready with their claws to serve death.
We turn to justice that it may quench the thirst,
that it nurse the wounds with magic ointments,
that would mend the torn flesh,
that would bring the dead back to life,
that would deliver eternal life.
The postmodern zoo blew up to destroy the colors.
Earthquakes have ruptured the island's pillars.
A few remaining hamburger carts survive,
the Koreans with their collection of multicolored fruit
and that solitary Black blowing a horn on Fifth Avenue.

Ma noi anneghiamo nell'East River,
senza speranze.
Noi penzoliamo impiccati dal Manhattan Bridge,
senza certezze.
Dilaniati dagli alligatori della palude
ci avviamo, sanguinanti, alla ricerca di un riparo.
È feroce Manhattan,
ultimo simbolo selvaggio di una civiltà alla deriva.

Yet we drown in the East River,
hopelessly.
We swing hanging from the Manhattan Bridge,
all certainty gone.
Mauled by the alligators in the marsh
and bleeding, we seek cover.
Manhattan is ferocious,
the last savage symbol of a civilization adrift.

DAL VENDITORE DELL'EMPORIO

Pinne. Ho bisogno di pinne.
Perché devo attraversare un oceano a nuoto.
Voglio un coltello. Per difendermi dai pescecani.
E una zattera, che mi salvi dalla deriva delle correnti.
E occhiali da sole con lenti spesse
per non vedere più il sole,
perché non mi accechi.
Dammi una vela che prenda il vento
verso un approdo sicuro.
Dammi una corda e un'ancora,
un'ancora, un'ancora salda,
che non si frantumi sugli scogli.
Acqua. Per non morire di sete.
E cibo. Per sopravvivere.
E un martello e chiodi e legno,
per costruire un riparo.
Lische di pesce
e solo poche conchiglie sparse,
dopo l'approdo,
celebreranno per sempre il naufragio.

THE SALES CLERK AT THE EMPORIUM

Flippers. I need flippers.
Because I have to swim across the ocean.
I need a knife. To protect myself from sharks.
And a raft, to save me from the tug of the currents.
And sunglasses with thick lenses
so I won't see the sun anymore,
so it won't blind me.
Give me a sail that takes to the wind
towards secure shores.
Give me a rope and an anchor,
an anchor, a solid anchor,
that won't shatter upon the rocks.
Water. So I won't die of thirst.
And food. To survive.
And a hammer and nails and wood
to build me a shelter.
Fishbones
and a few strewn shells
after the landing,
will celebrate the shipwreck forever.

TRAPPOLE

Per tre giorni è risuonato il corno della caccia.
E i cani hanno corso per dilaniare la volpe.
E gli arcieri hanno imbracciato gli archi
per trafiggere il cervo.
Con la pelle bruciata dal sole
i pescatori, impassibili, hanno inabissato le reti.
Trappole per topi
o per esseri umani.
Trappole.
L'agnello, ferito, è stato immolato.
Il cinghiale è crollato senza un lamento.
Il cigno si è adagiato sulla riva del lago, colpito a morte.
Tre giorni di caccia
per ritornare con la vittima nel carniere.
Solo tre giorni.
Per celebrare un banchetto di vittoria,
sul sangue.
La gazzella è inciampata
con le reti strette intorno ai garretti,
senza scampo.
Aveva corso. Non aveva più fiato.
Il cerchio si stringeva,
le corde la stritolavano.
Gli avvoltoi volteggiano sopra il Ponte di Verrazzano,
in direzione di Long Island.

TRAPS

For three days hunting horns blared.
The dogs raced to rip open the fox.
And the archers brandished the bows
to pierce the deer.
With sunburned skin
the fishermen, unmoved, drop the nets.
Traps for rats
or for human beings.
Traps.
Wounded, the lamb is sacrificed.
The boar is downed without a murmur.
The swan reclined on the lakeshore, lethally injured.
Hunting for three days
and returning with the victims in the gamebag.
Only three days.
To celebrate a victory banquet,
with blood.
The gazelle stumbles down
roped around the hocks,
it could not escape.
It had been running, it was out of breath.
The circle was getting smaller,
the ropes were chocking her.
The buzzards hovered above the Verrazano Bridge,
on the Long Island side.

VELENO

Ditemi chi ha versato un filtro magico nel mio vino,
chi ha trasformato in una visione di sogno
il profilo eclettico di New York.
Voglio sapere chi ha acceso lumini luccicanti
in tutte le strade del Village,
chi ha ricoperto di rose rosse i tavoli dei ristoranti.
Fatemi conoscere l'autore della colonna sonora,
il regista,
chi ha scritto i testi.
Ditemi chi ha scelto i costumi
e il cielo di cartone
e chi ha acceso una lampadina elettrica dietro la luna.
E per favore, per favore,
fate che io sappia il nome, il nome,
di chi ha portato il veleno sulla scena.
Veleno mortale nel mio cibo.
Veleno che ha gelato il sangue.
Membra paralizzate.
Ibernazione della mente e del cuore.
Un istante. È bastato un istante.
Veleno.

POISON

Tell me who poured a magic potion in my wine,
who changed New York's eclectic profile
into a dream vision.
I want to know who lit up bright little night lights
in all the streets in the Village,
who covered the restaurant tables with red roses.
I want to meet the author of the soundtrack,
the director,
the screenwriter.
Tell me who chose the costumes
and the cardboard sky
and who lit up a lightbulb behind the moon.
And please, please,
make sure that I know the name, the name,
of who brought poison on the set.
Deadly poison in my food.
Poison that froze my blood.
Paralyzed limbs.
Mind and heart in hibernation.
A second. It took only a second.
Poison.

ECLISSI AMERICANE

Il sole si è oscurato
e l'universo, immobile, ha smesso di respirare.
Tracce di buio inestricabile.
Presagi di gelo perenne.
E poi il nero incantesimo si è dipanato.
Il movimento ha trionfato sulla stasi.
L'energia ha travolto il silenzio.
La luna e il sole hanno ripreso le loro rotte.

Non ho più paura.
Il vento ha smesso di ululare.
La tempesta si è placata.
Sulle linee terse del paesaggio
si ridisegna il sorriso.
Avrò alberi e boschi e fiori
di cui inebriarmi.
E cavalli, per galoppare nel sole.
Avrò acque limpide in cui nuotare
ed infinite proiezioni planetarie
si disegneranno davanti ai miei occhi.
Avrò gatti accoccolati ai miei piedi
nelle notti d'inverno.
Raccoglierò fragole
e sentirò la freschezza della rugiada,
sull'erba, sotto i miei passi.

Non ho più paura.
Avanzerò imperterrita
in nebbie fitte ed acque turbolente.

AMERICAN ECLIPSES

The sun darkened
and the universe, motionless, stopped breathing.
Traces of inextricable darkness.
Omens of perennial ice.
And then the black spell unraveled.
Movement triumphed over stillness.
Energy ovverrun silence.
The moon and the sun returned to their course.

I am not afraid anymore.
The wind stopped wailing.
The storm subsided.
Against the terse lines of the landscape
a smile is drawn up again.
I will have trees and woods and flowers
to inebriate me.
And horses to gallop in the sun.
I will have clear waters in which to swim
and endless planetary projections
will outline themselves before my eyes.
I will have cats crouching at my feet
during winter nights.
I will pick strawberries
and feel the freshness of the dew
on the grass, under my steps.

I am not afraid anymore.
I will walk tall
amidst thick fogs and roiling streams.

Avrò paesi da visitare
e intere popolazioni da abbracciare.

Non ho più paura.
Ci sarà legna da ardere nel mio camino.
Avrò navi spaziali per crociere nelle galassie.
Camminerò su tappeti arabescati
e correrò contro vento, con forza.

Non ho più paura.
Il mondo mi appartiene
ed io appartengo al mondo.
È una simbiosi perfetta,
senza interferenze.
Le tempeste di mare
saranno onde dolci con cui giocare.
Gli uragani
solo deboli venti da governare.
Spegnerò incendi
come fossero candele.
E scioglierò la neve di tormente polari
col calore della mente.
E sentirò con gioia la morsa del sole
in estati torride,
senza bruciarmi.
E il buio non sarà un tunnel a senso unico
perché tutte le direzioni condurranno alla luce.
Nulla puó più temere
chi ha attraversato un'eclissi.

I have countries to visit
and whole populations I want to embrace.

I am not afraid anymore.
There will be wood to burn in my fireplace.
I will have spaceships for galactic cruises.
I will walk on arabesque carpets
and will run against the wind, with determination.

I am not afraid anymore.
The world belongs to me
and I belong to the world:
it's a symbiosis
without interferences.
Sea storms
will be sweet waves to play with.
Hurricanes
are mere winds to subdue.
I will put out fires
as if they were candles.
And I will melt the snows of polar blizzards
with the heat of my mind.
And I will feel the joy of the grip of the sun
in torrid summers
and not burn myself.
And the darkness will not be a one-way tunnel
because all signals point toward the light.
Nothing can frighten you anymore
if you have witnessed the eclipse.

Biographical Notes

FLAVIA PANKIEWICZ is a creative writer and freelance journalist born in Lecce of a Polish father and an Italian mother. She is the founding editor of *Bridge Apulia-USA*, an Italian-American magazine which she has edited since 1996. Contributor to the cultural page of *La Gazzetta del Mezzogiorno*, one of the main dailies in Southern Italy, she has written from and about the United States of America paying special attention to the subjects of literature and social issues.

She wrote for ten years for the most important Italian equestrian magazines and has also published a few biographies in *Cavalli e Cavalieri* (Milan: Rizzoli, 1981) and *Border to Border* (Milan: Ed. Equestri, 1988), a novel inspired by a true story.

PETER CARRAVETTA is Professor of Italian and Comparative Literature at the Graduate Center of the City University of New York and Head of the Faculty of European Languages and Literature at Queens College.

He is the founding editor of *Differentia. Review of Italian Thought* (1986). Translator and bilingual poet, he has written *Prefaces to the Diaphora. Rhetorics, Allegory, and the Interpretation of Postmodernity* (W. Lafayette: Purdue University Press, 1991), *Il Fantasma di Hermes* (Lecce: Milella, 1996) and *The Sun and Other Things* (Toronto: Guernica, 1997).